Neighbor Blood

Neighbor Blood

POEMS

RICHARD FROST

Sarabande Books

LOUISVILLE, KENTUCKY

FIRST EDITION

No part of this book may be reproduced without written
permission of the publisher. Please direct inquiries to:

Managing Editor
Sarabande Books, Inc.
2234 Dundee Road, Suite 200
Louisville, KY 40205

LIBRARY OF CONGRESS CATALOGING-IN-PUBLICATION DATA
   Frost, Richard, 1929–
      Neighbor Blood / Richard Frost. — 1st ed.
         p.   cm.
      ISBN 0-9641151-4-X (cloth : alk. paper).
      ISBN 0-9641151-5-8 (paper : alk. paper)
      I. Title.
   PS3566.R6N45   1996
   811'.54—dc20   96–4300
                                                          CIP

Cover Painting: *Jazz Musician,* 1958. By Larry Rivers. Oil on
canvas, 70" x 58". Private collection.
© 1996 Larry Rivers/Licensed by VAGA, New York, NY

Cover and Interior Design by Charles Casey Martin.
Text set in Sabon.

Manufactured in the United States of America.
This book is printed on acid-free paper.

Sarabande Books is a non-profit literary organization.

ACKNOWLEDGMENTS

The author gratefully acknowledges the following publications:

Abraxas/Chowder Review: "Clay"
The American Scholar: "The Edge of Something," "I Stroke My
    Sleeping Son," "Sen-Sen"
California Quarterly: "The Naked Eye"
Cimarron Review: "The Basket Case," "Winter Flies"
Esquire: "Animal Graves"
The Georgia Review: "The Old Hedonist's Dwindling Sestina"
The Gettysburg Review: "Cereal," "The Annunciation," "The
    Torturer's Horse"
Kenyon Review: "Fifteen"
Light Year '85: "The Clumsy Man"
The Literary Review: "New Tooth"
Massachusetts Review: "Collecting"
Mississippi Review: "On Durleston Road," "Reunion"
Negative Capability: "Words"
New England Review: "Storm"
The North American Review: "For a Brother"
The Paris Review: "The Change," "Neighbor Blood"
Poetry: "Marriage," "The Standing Broad Jump"
Poetry Miscellany: "A Small Story"
Poetry Northwest: "Winter Round"
Prairie Schooner: "You"
Raccoon: "Kisses"
Seneca Review: "The Hawk"
Shenandoah: "Line of Sight"
Slow Dancer: "The Family Way," "One Morning"
Western Humanities Review: "The Chamber," "Compare,"
    "Thebes Revisited"

Thanks to State Street Press for permission to reprint "Jazz for Kirby," to the Chester H. Jones Foundation for permission to reprint poems from their 1988 and 1989 anthologies, and to The Devil's Millhopper Press for permission to reprint poems from my chapbook *The Family Way.*

Thanks are due to the Yaddo Corporation for three residency fellowships, to the State University of New York for several summer writing fellowships, and to the National Endowment for the Arts for a creative writing fellowship.

for Daniel, Joel, and Cathy

CONTENTS

"For your soul," the Devil said, "one perfect poem."
"No," I said, "I'd rather do it myself."
So the Devil said, "All right, then, two poems."

Neighbor Blood

PART | One

Cereal

The little boy, fifty years ago, thinks that his cereal
from Battle Creek, Michigan, is somehow the serial
he likes to be scared by at Saturday matinees,
and the cowboys' checkered tablecloth is the same
as the Ralston cereal box with its red and white squares.
Words flicker and gallop like *Gun Battlers of Grim Creek*—
disappear, reappear, black hats, white hats,
white puffs of smoke, rifle fire, pistol fire.
The herd tumbles over the bank. Heard they robbed the bank!
Words have little smells, tastes. *Saw horses. Sea horses. Shoe trees.*
Shoo fly. Button your fly. Defense stamps. Offense, fence.
One nation invisible. Hot dog. Dogfight. Planes. Cross the plains.
Hangar. Clothes hanger. Pea. Pee. P. Polite. Light pole.
Today the ex-little boy learns that in Battle Creek
they turned to the breakfast cereal business,
invented grape nuts, early in the twentieth century
because the demand for animal feed was diminishing.
That's what makes him remember cereal and serial,
etc., and how one thing leads to another.
The grown man thinks now that maybe he has lost something,
that maybe now he's so sure of his words, that they mean
what they mean, that they *are* those same things,
that he's lost the feel, the texture, the little aromas
of words. *Baseball, bowl, bowel.* He doesn't really *hear*
the words, because they always mean something.
So the man goes around saying *train, traaain,*
training, rain, aviary. He walks his dog
and says *tree, three, three tree houses, mouse.*
He is so happy! He wraps his tongue
around the words. He tastes them. People look at him.
He gets out of his car and says *look, walk, watch,*
town, window, wind, windshield wiper.
He gets back into his car and turns on the wipers,

which scuff and squeal because it isn't raining.
He remembers the little song of the windshield wipers.
Saduffa, saduffa. More and more comes back.
He is a little boy again, sitting between his parents,
whose conversation makes no sense to him. *Pamphlet. Ambassador.*
He loves them. *Superintendent. Arbitrary.* He's going home.
You think he's likely to function well in this world?
You think he will? Would you bet your beans on him?
The cop is probably walking toward him right now.
He'll have trouble understanding anything seriously.
Serially. See? *Certainly. Central. Circle. Creek. Cereal.*

. . . even the dreadful martyrdom must run its course
Anyhow in a corner, some untidy spot
Where . . . the torturer's horse
Scratches its innocent behind on a tree.

AUDEN, *Musée des Beaux Arts*

The Torturer's Horse

It was almost as if the horse knew
it worked for an Old Master. Tied beside
the tree, it scratched its butt against the bark,
to suggest apathy, while the horse's owner,
chosen because he was the village baker
and had a comfortable paunch and otherwise
looked placid and ordinary, someone who'd never
even kick a cat, he stood beside his horse
modestly unpacking his kit of choking collars,
thumb screws and flaying knives. Those three kids
were rolling their hoops, and there was Peter
the smithy roped to a post and lifting his head
and howling like he knew just what he was in for.
I sat at a table in front of the inn,
my lips puckered, face to face with Hilda
the fat barmaid. All that innocence
while someone was about to be pulled apart
for choosing the wrong god.
                                      It went on for weeks,
until we'd all had it, even that fancy painter—
who had turned out to be a big pain in the ass,
had gotten stingy with the beer he'd promised
and probably never would have the fountain rebuilt—
was crabbing about the weather, the light changing,
and none of us looking commonplace enough.
The kids were tired of rolling hoops every day,
and of course there was the bread shortage. It was the horse
who first caused the problem. We'd taken a break

5

while the artist was mixing some paint
and cleaning brushes, and the horse reached down with his nose
and pushed over the box of torture instruments,
whereupon the baker, that blank, placid look
still in his eyes, kicked the horse hard enough
to make it stomp and whinny. Hilda leaned
into me and bit my lower lip,
and the kids threw down their hoops and began
tossing gobs of mud at the martyr, who twisted
out of his ropes and grabbed a pot of paint
and threw it at the feet of the Old Master,
who seemed at that point to decide he was wrong
about indifference. He painted a big X
across the unfinished picture and that afternoon
began the one he did finish, *The Village
Orgy*. It all bothered me so,
I went home and argued with my wife
until I had an excuse for beating her.
All it takes is proper illustration,
enough time, and someone to get it started.
Everyone's a torturer, except maybe a horse.

Storm

The father is tickling his six-year-old son.
He has the kid on the couch, on his back,
and keeps pushing him down. The father bends
over his son and works all over his middle
with both hands. Every once in a while
the father tweaks one knee or the other and makes
a noise, forcing air out between one cheek
and his gums, a sort of farting Donald Duck
noise. This makes the son laugh even harder
and try to kick the air, but the father holds down
the legs and then really starts digging
his fingers into the little boy's sides
and belly. Now it is hard to tell whether
the son is laughing or crying. His eyes have become
wide and full of tears, and they travel over
the ceiling and back to the father's face. "I'll pee,"
he says between whoops. "No. I'll pee. No."
"No you won't," says the father and keeps tickling
his son, who now is repeating "No" again
and again and still laughing and crying and shaking
his head, wildeyed, and the father says,
"No way my boy will pee in his pants," as the wet
stain spreads across the son's trousers
and the father stops the tickling. "You're still a baby,"
he says and picks up the kid by one arm
and yanks him off of the couch. "Look at this mess,"
the father says and pulls off the bottom panel
of the upright piano and pushes the boy inside,
cramming him in there and snapping the panel shut.
"Listen to this," says the father, pounding up and down
the keyboard with his fists. "You're a baby,
you're a baby," the father chants, drowning out
the struggle inside the piano. Soon, his wife

comes into the room. "What was all that noise?"
she asks. "You woke me up, playing the piano.
I thought you were taking care of Sonny."
"Never mind," says the father, grabbing her
by the neck, dragging her down beside him
onto the couch. "Never mind that sissy. I'll
show you how a real man operates."
A rain storm begins outside, hissing on the porch.
Bursts of light flood the yard. Framed in the windows,
the trees seem to leap in the air, and a terrible cracking
and rumbling fills the world, the house at its center.
All the while, through the wire screens,
a sweet mist enters the room. He begins
pulling off his shirt and looks in her eyes
with kindness past her best imaginings.
Brushing his lips gently with the back of her hand,
she tells him about the storm, how much it affects her,
and as they make love they both understand
what it is like to be swept along by a storm,
to be set into motion and then to keep going. As the storm
in the room settles, the son inside the piano
uncovers his ears, braces himself, and with both heels
forces open the panel and rolls onto the floor.
He stands, walks past his sleeping parents and out
the door. There, on the concrete steps, he sees
the wet and empty street, the trees and clouds.
Low behind the hills, faint thuds and flashes
trace the storm. He stares at the senseless sky,
then looks away, down the long tunnel
of unnatural law, into his own life.

Neighbor Blood

Park Ridgeway's wife, this hot August afternoon,
comes shrieking across the street with one hand
over her left eye, beats on the front door,
and Skipper the Jack Russell terrier
goes hysterical, yapping and yodeling
and springing at the curtains and tearing them.
Just fine, just fine, my old man keeps saying,
and she's there in the kitchen with a wet washcloth
over the swollen eye and crying and bending over
and then it really starts. I'm a little kid,
so I'm no help. What do I know? My mother
is running cold water on another washcloth
and folding it into a smaller square and trading
washcloths and then you can hear these big feet
on the porch, and hollering, and I run into the front
hallway behind my father, and Ridgeway smashes
his fist through our leaded glass window
beside the front door and reaches around inside
and yells you bastards. So my father takes Ridgeway's
wrist in both hands and just cranks his arm
in a circle, then pushes it right down
onto the edge of the broken window glass,
and that's basically the end of this story
because I went upstairs and got in my closet.
They're all dead anyway, and it's a long time
since that neighbor blood was wiped up
and dried up and it went back into basic atoms
and molecules and, who knows, maybe it's part
of my blood now, or yours, or part of anybody's.

The Chamber

In Dresden, East Germany,
nervous and thrilled behind the Iron Curtain,
there on a camping trip with my wife and two children,
we four on a busy, strange sidewalk, red banners
flying above us, I had to go to the toilet.
At the intersection I saw the familiar 00 sign
and a dark stairway leading down. I found

at the foot a rank and ancient room of stone,
a trough around the edge. An iron grate
in the far ceiling shed the only light.
Trying not to breathe, I stood at the trough
where Goethe must have stood a time before,
and cleared myself of a midday liter of beer,
zipped up and turned to leave. And then I caught

a movement in the squalid shadows
not far away. My adjusted eyes
were drawn to two old men who paid no heed
to me. One's tattered overcoat was wrapped
partly around his friend, whose pendent hand
moved inside the first one's open fly.
I saw it in a moment, all of it,

and hurried out. In the fetid underground
beneath the traffic's rumble and what I took
in my simple truth to be the daily rounds
of the subjects of a captive state,
two grizzled men were looking deep into
each other's eyes with such accord
that nothing mattered—least of all, me.

Marriage

First, it was the common magic—
organdy skirt, lace petticoat,
your hair in sunlight,
our tight young skin.
Our act was applauded,
held over, licensed in May.

I grew adept at pulling spring blossoms
out of a glass. Bushels of them lay
around your ankles. I learned the rising cards,
the inexhaustible bottle. A toy bird perched
at the top of my chair, fluttering and warbling.
On a table my brazen head of Orpheus
clanked and answered questions. For encore I drank
a melted mixture of pitch, brimstone and lead
from an iron spoon, the stuff blazing furiously.

With my rings, levers and spindles, gears and hoops,
sockets, springs and bellows, I became famous.
The apparent floating of a woman in empty space
was my best. I covered an iron lever with velvet
matching the background and therefore invisible.
The lever, attached to a socket in your metal girdle,
passed through an opening in the back curtain.
You rose, spinning, fanning the air like a bird.
Then I passed a hoop over your body
and brought you to the floor.

11

Taking from my pocket a newspaper,
I opened it and laid it upon the stage.
I showed the audience a chair, front and back,
and placed it on the paper. You took your seat,
and I cast over you a piece of black silk.
I shouted, "I'll throw you in the air,"
grasped your waist and lifted you above my head.
You vanished, covering and all, at my fingertips.

The Edge of Something

A dream of Halloween, the walls
orange and black in the retarded light
of the gas lamps. On the stones
a truck crosses, three blocks away,
then a car with soldiers. Nothing.
Burning coal. A latticed window with vines.
In the yellowed Gasthaus, the dead ones are helped away.
The angry butcher gives us his recipe for Bratwurst.
Strangers roll their eyes, their heads pivot.
A waiter prances out. We are led
along a slim roadway, with the moon huge.
We walk on the edge of something. A Strassenbahn,
its front end black except for a milky eye,
waits, empty. We cross in front of it, it clangs,
and we climb on, back toward that place
where we have what the good are given.

A Small Story

In this cold place, where the light drains away
at four in the afternoon, she stood by this gate,
whoever she was, and looked at the plum tree until
she knew it had become her vanished husband,
or he had become it. She stood here crying pitifully,
seeing his branches turned upward that should hold her,
yet she stayed inside the gate, afraid to caress
the hardened nerve and blood, the cold hide
he had put on. Afraid, one might suppose,
he would take her to his black, sodden bed
gladly, if she dared touch the bark.
So she stood here wishing as hard as she could,
again and again and again, to make him resume
his proper flesh. And stubbornly he held firm,
lifting his limbs to her. Finally
she died and was put into the churchyard.
The story never is done with that.
Each time, the teller laughs and adds
that most husbands and wives are finally at such distance.
And certainly he had gone to another village
to marry again. And she was only crazy.
Yet they keep telling the story.

The Basket Case

During the war, in high school, I first heard it.
Only a few, the story went, were wounded
so terribly. No stumps to attach
anything to. I imagined it all a lie.

Last night I saw pictures of a man
rigged in an electric harness of levers and arms
and buttons to press with his chin. He ran a business
over the telephone, supported a family,

touched a special typewriter with a stick
held in his teeth. Poured himself a beer.
Strapped in his robot chair, he went to games.
Science and a will to live had given him

the joy that a few years earlier had seemed
impossible. I imagined it a lie.

Kisses

When Edna, our cleaning lady, arrives, she kisses
our golden retriever full on the mouth, holding
his head in her hands and rubbing her lips
back and forth against his, maybe even
french kissing him. She moves back a half inch
and murmurs, in a voice so amorous that though
she is very ugly, probably even too ugly for the dog,
it raises the hairs on the back of my neck,
and the dog braces his legs and looks
sideways and up at me. "My baby," she croons.
"My baby, how have you been this week?
I have some scraps for you." What interests me most
is that the dog, Zachary, is clearly embarrassed.
When she lets go to reach into her purse
for the meat, he stays in the kissing posture, his eyes
rolling around to mine. "Get me out of this,"
I think he says. She lays the meat on the floor,
and he stares at it and then looks at the wall.
"Don't worry 'bout the floor, baby," she says.
"That's what I'm here for. Lie down and eat."
When was the last time I kissed a dog?
I think, and of course it all comes back. I kissed
my first several thin-lipped dogs,
my own dogs, my puppies, fuzzy sweet
mouths, licking me, generous, my eyes and ears,
and my mother somewhere else and no washing.
My first private love. Now, though I have read
that dogs' mouths have fewer germs than mine,
I think, *Fewer, but maybe worse,* and I
cannot go beyond touching my nose to the dog's.
"Maybe his mother told him not to kiss people,"
I say to Edna. "He's shy and serious,"
she says. Zachary, hearing the voices, lies down

16

and eats the scraps. "I got a dog home,"
she says. "My old man says I'm crazy. But I,
I don't know where I could get anything better."

Jazz for Kirby

"Now, you gotta get up on the beat.
Like, there's *four* beats, see? That's the *beat*.
Some drummers hit right on the beat, and
some a hair after. You gotta get just up,

"not like right *over* the beat, but onto it
just a little, on its front edge. See,
it's like you have these four chicks lookin' at you.
Man, you don't wanna jump right on top of them.

"Just nudge real pretty. That way you lift.
You lift, I mean. Man, and you do it without
getting any faster. Or any louder. Keep that pedal
right there—bum, bum, bum, bum,

"exactly on the beat, and then lift
with the sticks and hi-hat. You *establish*
the beat with your bass drum, and then you
keep those ladies right there

"and you do those pretty things to *elev*ate everyone.
Guy comes in off the street, he can't see you yet,
he can't even *hear* the drums, but he can feel it.
He knows you're there. Big Sid was the best.

"He could hit the cymbals with handkerchiefs
and drive a whole band. He could hit one cymbal.
It's not how *many* drums or how loud.
It's your lift. Tic-a-tah, tic-a-tah, *zit,*

"I mean. A dup, a-dup-a and a-dup-a *zit* tah.
Like when it's a-poppa poppa pie, baby, you carry everything.

Now get your ass up there on that stool.
This time we're *going* to *do* it."

All teeth, scotch & soda in his fist,
he bows at the upright. Elbow, chin. The idea
to cripple himself in as many ways as he can
and still hit the piano. One leg over his shoulder,

mouth full of white keys, he blinds
the drunks. I putter beside him, keeping
just up on the beat, as if someone
listened through the thunder, as if

I had the real message. The glasses rattle
like xylophones in Jerry's. A salesman lays
two dollars on the red velvet, and Kirby's face
bulges. Music is business.

"See the lady with the *red* dress on,"
he sings, two handfuls of keys.
I have to know every break so I can forget it.
Show time! Kirby yells, and I play my press roll.

No lights and a spot but still no one
but "Mother Macree" from somewhere, and on walks
Kendall the black Irish tenor,
clear and insolent. Once someone says

Kendall has no right to sing that way,
and Kendall says he'd better
not ever hear that white mouth singing blues.
Kirby stays polite and slightly stooped

on the job. Roll-up eyes. Teeth.
Kendall can tell anyone
fuck himself but doesn't know jazz.
Kirby got born just right for one thing,

too soon for another. At his house
he stands straight. On the stand
he's Old Man Shuffle. Yeh! Ah know!
Kendall raises his arms

and threads "Danny Boy" like silver
over that roomful of white money
he frightens into believing him.
"What you guess I showed those mothers?"

Late on a slow night, Kirby says,
"This one's dedicated to *us.*"
Twenty minutes of "Just You, Just Me"
with all my choruses lined up,

Kirby leering down the keys at me,
no stupid requests to bother us,
Kirby growling, "Richie, be pretty.
Don't fall on those ladies."

"I'm gonna have you all fixed up," says Kirby.
"What?" "See that waiter? I know him.
We'll set you up with a black chick.
You need your ashes hauled."

Kirby's toupee is slightly skewed.
We are at Small's Paradise.
"Twenty-five bucks, there's a beautiful chick in your room.
I know you have this nice background.

"You had a mother and father, right?
Lots of nice bread. Don't fix your face up, now, man!
Look at me! Look at your leader, now!
Get your eyes up. I'm trying something for you.

"Everybody needs to learn, man. You're a professor,
but you have not got the corner
on making things go. I showed you Fats Waller's piano.
I *tried* to teach you rhythm. Fessor,

"you chic-a-tic along like Mickey Mouse,
but I think you got something better. Anyway,
you the only drummer I got in that town.
How about we take that broomstick up your back

"and elasticize it? I don't put you down, man.
I like you. Richie Forest on the drums!
But don't be stiff. When you go back to your room,
there's coming on your door a knock-knock."

Shuffling my poems, I wait for the knock.
Beautiful black chick.
"Listen, come in. You want to hear a poem?"
"Shee . . . , *what* you got there? *Poem?*"

"Yes, I'm a poet. Here's a book of my poems."
"Thirty dollars, I'll listen to you fucking poems."
"They said it was twenty-five." "No, man, it's always thirty."
"How about twenty-five and a signed copy of my book?"

"Twenty-eight and you don't have to sign."
"Twenty-six fifty and just my initials."
I spread the money across the top of the dresser,
and she feeds it into her purse.

Wearing the chauffeur hat, Kirby is steering
his big green Jaguar. He has me in back.
"Did she trick you nice? Don't brag, now.
I knew you was a tomcat. Do you know

"what's a tomcat? A tomcat's a ball-bearing
mouse trap. Man, when I tell you
what's good, that's it! If I say
go over a fence backward, that's because

"then you don't tear your pants. Man, I played
for King George. I wore white gloves
with a big ring on each finger. I gave him
the flash, lift my hands way up,

"and he is very deeply moved. Looka these cats
look at you, Richie! They think you're rich!
I'm gonna sing you about the bow-legged woman
with the red dress on. It's blues, man.

"There's nothin' without the blues. Everybody
has blues, and when you don't play them,
you don't know anything. Just a simple four bars
on this C chord, and then F and C

"and G and F and C again. That's the start!
That's boogie too! You turn the corners
real nice, those changes, oooh-eeee,
it's so pretty. But you gotta know where it's at

"before you leave it. No horns screamin',
running the sequences, all the ladies'
fingers in their ears! Just you and me
and the blues, Richie. I know I cotton

"to all them swells. 'I know that you know.'
I *know* I gotta live successful. Man, I can't
turn my act into a sit-in like Kendall.
Anyway, he's got just the one thing.

"But there's a world in those funky blues.
You don't need a whole lot of goddam noise.
Pres said once, they want everybody who's a Negro
to be an Uncle Tom or Uncle Remus or Uncle Sam.

"You know civil rights wrecked my band?
Man, we played all over the North.
Then, all of a sudden there's no place to go.
Those cats didn't *want* Negro business.

"So I came upstate and built a house
myself, and I got a bad liver.

Slam, Buster, all those guys
come see me sometimes, but it ain't New York.

"I gotta tell you it's always a trade-off
wherever you go. Down at the Copper Rail
you see all the cats, drink a lot of that
idiot water, have a good time, all the gigs

"you get when your face is in the right place.
I might go back before they forget me.
I'd like to cut some sides again, Richie.
But next thing I knew I'd be heading back here.

"I get down there playing, I'm in one hotel
and another. I don't have no home
in New York, and I come back here.
But I been there, Richie. I went everywhere.

"So, listen, you just concentrate it all down
into twelve measures, all secret and pretty.
Lotsa lift, little nudge around the corners,
singin' about that bow-legged lady."

PART | TWO

Winter Flies

At eighty she had narrowed life to a box
of family pictures. Each day she worked deeper,
annotating: *Byran Dickersen,*
my uncle, in uniform of a Knight Templar.
Notice how his eyes resemble mine.

That same month the winter flies
fell on her like spent bullets.
They popped against the pictures as she found
her son's eyes, or her own, or her daughter's mouth
on her father in his garden cutting roses.

The flies struggled in her hair or whirred at the light.
They gathered on their backs in the window jambs.
Like her people, they were everywhere.
The Hogans crowded along the running board
of a Maxwell with wooden spokes, labeled *Denver.*

Colonel Grigsby with his rod of white beard.
Liza Jane with her diphtheria.
In the attic thousands of flies
were walking, their wings held close. A pest control
had told her they were in the house forever.

She worked her way through the box and taped it closed
and marked it *Save.* Presently she died.
The new people had no trouble killing the flies.
Their first winter they left for three months
and boarded up the house and let it freeze.

I Stroke My Sleeping Son

I stroke my sleeping son to comfort myself.
Saintly in the dark, I mope. My father's
nails, when he lay swathed in plastic tubes,
dug at my hand three times, and then he failed.
And yet I held his fist and waited for
the yielding up of his unstrangled soul.

Here in my son's dark I tell myself
my hand grows like my father's more each day,
and with it now I touch the quiet child,
my knuckles warm, my fears almost mislaid
until they find me out, stone on my chest,
my son awake. He makes my hand his own.

Animal Graves

Her jaws clamped on the little body, she calls
from deep in her throat to her kittens, explaining,
"We are cats, and this
is a mouse." She lets them poke the gray
dead fur and limp neck. "We kill mice."

We watch with her, but my children, remembering
their heritage of mice in the cartoons,
carry the body politely by the tail
out of the room. A Kleenex box
filled with cotton makes a long coffin.

When I wore bicycle clips,
I put my dead in a row behind the fence.
A dog, a canary, turtle and cat, with mounds
and coat-hanger crosses, baked in the sun
until the rains washed away everything.

Today, shallow in the iris bed,
is a mouse in a paper carton. My pets
cross the rug, stretch out by the fire
until they are flat. A ceiling of roots
rubs them. They speak with the blades of summer.

First Haircut

You are perched on a padded board
on the arms of the barber's chair, your curls
adrift on the floor, your mother quietly
twisting her blue handkerchief
as you sit face-to-face and back-to-back
in the mirrors forever, your new forehead shining.
Does she see your father, hers, his father
in the glass, back and back in the long room
where you sit in your sheet and tissue collar
while the barber clips you bare?

Why remember it now, fifty years
after, sitting across from her doctor
and signing a paper? Is it the white room?
Is it the deep, secret delight that you
are the last alive? When the nurse lays
the gold wedding band on the desk and you read
the initials inside and the room
smells of bleach and alcohol,
your mother wrapped in a sheet, the barber
spinning his chair, shaking a towel, why
think now of the mirrors that travel forever?

Line of Sight

How true the corner of the tv
lines up with the dog's ear and the lamp
when I hold my head just so. In San Francisco
once I caught myself sighting a line
between one nipple of a go-go girl
and a plastic philodendron behind the bar.
One eye shut, I leaned half off my stool.

In the drafting room the dead engineer
bristles with pens and protractors, cranking a beast
that thumps its heavy carriage at the top of its keys,
his maps squared off like the whole Midwest.
If I make a sound, he will throw a t-square at me,
so I sight across the brim of his Adam hat.

As soon as he dies, they burn him down to ash
as he has ordered, and pour him into a box
and fly him out beyond the three-mile limit
where the pilot, like a bombardier,
releases him into a perfect curve.

He showed me how to get somewhere, and now
my chair is parallel with my walls and my floor
and my roof and my walk and the street before my house
and everything straight, measure beyond measure
as far as it goes, reason telling me flatly
about safety in numbers, about fine lines
between ocean and vision, drowned and deep image,
the purest fountain and the weakest ending.

The Naked Eye

First came the large bushy floaters,
out of focus, sailing left when I turned my eyes
right, then coming all the way back
when I looked left, meeting me at dead center.
Next, the dark specks—
periods, commas, beauty marks and a blackbird
hovering at the edge of the paper I wrote on
or riding a corner of the Buick's windshield.
The specks and big floaters came and went,
but the bird was always there. Then the flashes
at the rim of sight, like toy flashlights
from Christmas dreams. For nights their incandescences
heralded the gray half moon that rose one morning
as I groped toward a hall of shadows.
"You have a detached retina,"
my doctor murmured as he drew a picture.
"I won't let you leave this hospital
before I do something. A scleral buckle,
a band of silicone sewn around the eyeball.
We relocate your retina, and it's there for good."
The compact, crewcut anesthesiologist
in green sleeves like a lightweight wrestler
touched my wrist with a needle and I woke
in a red pulsing world of sheets and ceilings
and bedrails and no gray moon—but there
in the cinched vision of my recovered morning,
forever, off my left wing,
was the sharp-eyed, patient blackbird
flying toward darkness.

The Clumsy Man

Well, I am clumsy. I stumble, I hit my head
on chandeliers. I'm a tall, clumsy man.
I miss my mouth with my food, I fall out of bed,
I forever bite my cheek or else my tongue.

The woman I love has learned to be wary near me
lest I turn suddenly and put my elbow
into her teeth or deep in her dear kidney.
We kiss and my forehead knocks against her brow.

Unless I am careful, careful, careful,
I drive over the curb or crack my wine glass.
I have tied my left shoe to my right
and dropped a baby. All of it will pass.

When the choir sings over my perfumed bones,
I will cough until I am asked to leave.
I will step on my undertaker's toe,
lurch through his oak door and, farewell, feel

sweet symmetry around my open wings.

Reunion

Lifting the little box of your ashes, I tell
the mortician I've heard they can't burn

everything. "What about teeth
and the hard bones?" I ask him. "Are they in here?"

"Everything's there," he says. "We run it through the crusher,
all the big stuff. Now it's a fine powder."

I push you into my knapsack, my pulverable father,
and ride home on the bus with you on my lap.

When were we so close?
You drift in your clammy room,

all that cannot ascend,
and we're under one roof.

One Morning

My brother's wife phones me and says I'd better drive over
right away for what will probably be the last visit,
so I get in my mother's old Buick and two hours later
I'm at their apartment at Smugglers' Village in Stockton.
My brother's life has been a mess all along.
He came out of the war a drunk, lost on the horses,
failed in real estate and fiction writing,
and has held briefly one good job after another.
He is alternately charming and a bully, and I probably
wouldn't be his friend if he were not my brother.
Now he is dying of brain cancer. The surgeons
have removed an apricot-sized tumor from the back
of his head. He has regained the power of speech,
but is dying fast. Here I find him standing
at the door, in his brown leather jacket
and the blue knit sailor's cap to hide his baldness.
No one has told him that he is going to die,
and like everyone else he believes he will live forever.
The first thing he tells me is that he has gained two pounds.
On his way back! He told his doctor to turn off the switch
if they couldn't get the whole tumor. His doctor
let him wake up, so that means they took out the cancer,
and now he will have a long, gradual recovery,
which is all a "hell of a problem." He is six feet tall
and weighs in at a hundred and twelve. Do I want some Scotch?
Back in the kitchen, his wife flits to and fro,
fixing a sandwich. She has hidden her bottles
for twenty years in the laundry basket,
behind the canned preserves and under the dresser.
She can't remember things. Their little terrier
Packy hysterically yaps, rattling his claws
on the picture window, jumping down from the couch
and skidding into the kitchen. Do I want some Scotch?

Yes. And we talk about the war, our father,
the cars we've owned, the family fishing vacations.
My brother's skin is yellow, and his eyes
are a very clear blue. He remembers the time
he was on the Ralph Edwards television show
This is Your Life, because he'd been a friend
of the Chicago policeman whose life this was. We talk
about this for a half hour. Do I want
more Scotch? Yes. His wife brings sandwiches
and three capsules for my brother. I am not making sense
because the dog wants out and my brother's wife
is back there crying, and finally what I remember
is our laughing about something. My brother and I
laugh about something he did. It is about
the time he faked an earthquake, or ate the ant
crawling along the drainboard, or stole the chair
from the restaurant. I will never remember exactly
what it is we laugh about, but we laugh.
Then I drive home, across the bay
in the evening. It makes no sense at all.
I come home, and my brother's wife is right
about that being the last visit.

Words

When you lost your words, you wrote,
"I asked him to be honest last of the long work
that I'm done or win. Best man in the country
I find out is my man. He will look my head
over again about tomorrow and cut me some
four or five hours Friday. It hurts me
but if I go in awhile maybe I can find Dad."

Once, in spring, in 1941,
the rain woke me at three a.m.,
and I ran to your bed. We never could go fishing
in such weather, I cried in your arms. You told me
to get to sleep, the rain would be gone in the morning.
We hiked in sunlight into the Butano,
each leaf a mirror. Pool to cold pool,
we traveled along the river. Trout in my creel.
You left to fight the Germans in Italy.

"Years to be together and see the house,"
you wrote. "I thought I'd be around for twenty years.
Now I think I might be first. I love you so.
We laugh that is so filling."

                    I'm the head
of this family now, my mother says.
When I drive my roads you never saw,
I whisper to you what you ought to see.
We can fish tomorrow, but today
I want to show you where I work. Tonight
we'll drink together and talk about the cars
and the girls and the football games and trout.

"They took my head apart," you said, bald
as Warbucks from the cobalt. Your leather jacket,
your wool cap. "I'm weak as spaghetti," you said,
"but I've got my words again."
A month of clear words and a stitched-up head.

A rattler coiled in the trail, too still. You touched it
with the tip of your pole. Someone had killed it
and put it there to scare us, or someone else
with a bad heart. Stupid trick, you said.
I followed along the best stream in the world.
Most of the world was wild. Salmon eggs
on my hook. Egg sandwiches. A dragonfly
cruising the top of the water. Now the river's
behind someone's back fence and full of soap.

You lost your Army savings at the track,
wrecked two company cars and beat your wife
and drank good whiskey till you couldn't stop.
You got fired and bought a boat.
You tallied your women and claimed there'd been two hundred
spread-eagled under you. You tried to write
stories about yourself that would make big money.
You shelled out to an agent who advertised.
"My agent," you said.

Finally you saw our father float
into the corner of the television screen.
"That's Dad right there," you said. "Right at the edge."
They wired up your mouth and hired a priest
who tried to sell us something while you smiled
in your box of silk. Afterwards I drove
our mother's Buick half across the state

and back to its garage and dragged down the door
and walked inside and washed and had a beer.

Here's my fishing spot. Lightning threw
that tree across the stream. In that shadow
I caught three trout for breakfast yesterday.
"I can't remember," you wrote. "Or get to my words."
We'll take this path, brother, up the bank,
across the pasture, through the thorn apples,
over the fallen wall, and find my house.
Like two old friends met in an underworld,
we'll tell our best stories half the night
as if forgetting what is lost, as if
one never could lose what he had to say.

For a Brother

When I was young, there was a song that went,
"I told you that I love you, now get out."
Last night, drunk at my party, you knocked over
the gas grill and blackened swordfish, you lout,
then tried to feel up my neighbor's daughter.
You sick rantallion, you phone at four a.m.
with a new joke, or to brag, or to beg for a loan.

Young, I didn't know what that song meant.
It just seemed funny. Today I am
bone tired of the crude fraternal weight
of your old bullying, you jackalone,
you sack of black rats' balls, you tank of piss.
And yet I love you, and so I must wait
until you're dead before I publish this.

The Family Way

The actors are grouped at one end of the stage,
their eyes wide and hollow, waiting for me
to put words in their mouths. They look at each other
and waggle their heads. They hold their arms
out wide at their waists, their palms upward.
Their lips make circles. Across the floor
I am writing fast, the pages rising
before me. "Dialogue," they say, mouthing
silently the word. They form a tight circle,
staring inward. In the second row
of the darkened theater sits the director, his brow
tapping the back of the seat before him. So I write
what could have happened. Beside me on the stage
my mother, my father, my brother, my aunt, my grandparents
seat themselves at a table. My father carves
a roast. My mother serves carrots and peas. My brother
pours wine for everyone and raises his glass.
"Here's to Dick," he says. "We miss him so."
As the actors drain their glasses, the house lights come on,
and the director screams, "That's terrible!
We all know the kid dies last." The actors leave
the stage, and I walk to the table and find
my place. Around me the full plates grow cool
as the lights come down. I set paper before me,
my back to the empty house, and write: *I am home. . . .*
Everyone else has left. What next?

The Old Hedonist's Dwindling Sestina

The silken rituals of pleasure,
fashioned for the practiced eye, I have
held them, felt them return and return
until it could only seem that time
itself was asking me for mercy,
that I not fill it so with all my

tasted hours, my raised voices, my
epic odysseys of pleasure.
How long have I known the mercy
of the most ardent calling, had
it ebb and then, in quickened time,
come but to its own returning?

The whispers that would return,
the loyal feastings, all my
sweet fabrics of bolted time,
long yardages of pleasure,
rooms, miles, everything I have
laid before my own mercy,

now a stranger mercy
hesitates to return.
Although I see I have
eye, ear, tongue, nose, all my
skin and more, my pleasures
have wandered off in time.

All of life is time,
all joy its mercy,
all death its pleasure

that it may return
to life,—and yet *my*
time is all I have.

Is what I've had
the most that time
could give to me
in its "mercy,"
so it must turn
off my pleasure?

Have mercy,
Time! Return
my pleasure.

Winter Round

Deep in the town the cold gong
of the church reminds us day and night
of the churchyard's congregation straight
under a windy song.

The winds play in the hard limbs
a song that turns those in the church
toward bared oak and peeling birch
out from the warm hymns.

There the trees with polished spines
against the air that sets them to crack
stand root to root and back to back
whistling their stiff tunes.

You

Know well that despite what is new
in dress or manners, I drank the same full
cup you would, and my smooth belly
warmed in the sun like any part of you.
My fields, never a stale grainy picture,
rolled and stuck to me. I heard snow,
smelled lightning, kissed every now
and then. And then when I was sure
what I touched was real, it had already been.
Mostly, I believed in what I saw.
What didn't exist was the past, and I saw it grow
out of my ripe days and immediate plans.
You know it all. Rub your white teeth
with your tongue. Hear your sweet breath.

PART | **Three**

Collecting

"Get in, I need to go see Whittell.
He hasn't paid." The Chandler bucked
out the driveway, one wheel over the curb,
my father rigid behind the wooden wheel;
puttees, work shoes, blue coat and vest;
reeking of tobacco and belches. "The chiseler
hasn't paid. We'll get it. You want a Hershey bar?"
"Yes." "O.K., after we see Whittell. Here."
We lurched down the long drive, and two dogs
dogged the car. A child in a sack dress
put her hand in her mouth as my father ran over
one dog and banged the other. "You hit the dogs!"
"What dogs? Whittell isn't here." He wheeled
around the circle before the house and out
again past the staring girl and now her brother.
"Those dogs, Dad." "Listen, do you want
a Hershey bar?" "Yes." "All right, then."

And I tore the brown wrapper the color of chocolate
and opened the white paper and bit,
and loved the sweet juice,
and my father grinned,
and we were alone together.

On Durleston Road

Here, by the letter box,
is where the white dog lay

guarded by a large dog sitting
with his head down, growling seriously,

looking at no one. The dead dog,
face in the gutter, was approached by many,

who backed from the bowed growling head.
The pound man's gray truck

came alongside, and the loyal dog, seeing
the wire cage, went slowly down the sidewalk,

looking back around his shoulder.
No. When the dead dog's legs

ran as if it were dreaming, the other dog
leaned over it and licked its face.

Then the cold soft belly began to assume
some terrific life of its own,

the dog stiffened and chattered, its pupils
turned white, and it lifted to its feet,

its face teeming, and it turned to the other dog,
who walked slowly away, down the sidewalk,

looking back around his shoulder.
I wish I could get it straight.

Anyway, that big-headed mongrel
like the Victor dog with his head down

did sit for part of an afternoon
growling beside a dead dog

and then walked off for some reason,
looking back at me

around his shoulder.
That's bad enough.

Drummer Remembers MacQuinn

Mr. MacQuinn, conducting our class
in singing the *Marines' Hymn,* unfailingly
skipped a measure at the end
of every phrase. It nearly

drove me nuts—that wire-haired Scot
would lead us with his little wand:
"To the shores of Tripoli we fight
our country's battles on the land

and on the sea first to fight . . . ,"
and the whole class as dumb about counting
as their mentor. "Wait for the rest! ' . . . the sea,'
(one-*two!)* 'First to *fight,*'" I yelled and got sent

out of the room. Now it's much later.
I am a drummer and I am called
for a pickup job, home town, and there
sits MacQuinn, wrinkled and bald

and playing sax with a bow-tie smile.
I could relent, I know, and say
that in the sea of forms he has found
truth, good, and beauty and learned to play

so that the universal grace
shines from his eternal core.
But art is partly craft, and MacQuinn
comes in too soon the same as before.

New Tooth

"This will be good material for you,"
says my dentist, pointing to the surprise
of mirrors rigged so that I can watch him
cut the top off of one of my molars
and hollow the stub and build a new tooth.
He rubs his sore back. "Why in hell aren't you watching?"
he says. "This is art too." I squint at the blood
as he lifts out pieces and drills the pink center.
"There's nothing better," he says. "I make you a tooth
harder than the real one. Exactly the right color.
It works and it's pretty and it becomes part of you.
That's art," he says. I have a mouth
full of clamps and cotton and hoses that suck
saliva. I could otherwise say something
about the tooth having no one's name on it
and how if my dentist dies and I forget
which tooth it is and if I die,
where then is art? But then I think of Hamlet
holding my skull. "Alas, poor Frost! I never
knew him, Horatio, but . . . Will you look at that tooth!"
I may be a dark gallery of one work
by an aching sculptor. "Uh-huh, uh-huh," I say
with my dead jaw. "Don't move," he says.
"Don't try to talk. Just watch." Then
he straightens, flexes an arm and rubs
the small of his back with the other hand.
"My life's work is killing me," he says.
"I wonder sometimes whether I ought to find
a job I could do without bending over."
"Uh-huh," I say, and in the mirrors,
my senseless tongue aquiver, I watch his hands
resume their carving. His little instruments
flash inside my mouth. He says, "Most people

wouldn't care to do this sort of thing.
But you've got to try to build something."
"Uh-uh-uh," I say. "Uh-huh. Uh-huh."

Fifteen

Late that summer my girlfriend's boyfriend
came home from a year in the merchant marine
blond and tanned and drove her away
in his cut-down souped-up '36 Ford.
On the swinging sofa in her back yard
my hand had strayed down her dress and she
had straightaway promised that henceforth we
were nearly married and never would part.
Now she was parked on a hill above town
with that tattooed bastard and I had no car.

I'd blow him sky high with a match in his tank,
I promised, and walked to her house. In the hedge,
doubled up, I waited half the night
with her purring cat that lifted its chin
to be scratched. The cat was all I had left.
Then, with the radio blaring "Moonlight and Roses,"
they coasted up, both in the driver's seat.
I crouched while her mother blinked the porch light,
and my lost Nancy jumped out of the car,
skipped up to her door, and the cat ran in.

The little twin taillights disappeared down the street,
and the house went dark. What should I do?
I backed carefully out of the hedge,
ducked to the sidewalk, and sank my fists
deep in my pockets. Where could I walk
but home? And whom could I tell how the moon,
who had been featured in my songs
until I thought he rhymed with love,
was a yellow sphere with some blue shadows,
above the trees, moving across the sky?

Sen-Sen

Those tiny black chips that corrected my breath,
where are they? In a small factory
in western Pennsylvania are two men
still baking the formula, tweezing each flake
into those envelopes? I can't find it
anywhere—not on the stock exchange,
not way in the back of my old bureau drawer
or in the lining of my tux. Where is Sen-Sen?
Two of those little squares and I'd be dancing
with girls in the gym, my feather carnation
wired to my lapel, the dance band swinging
those Miller stocks. I'd smell hair and gardenias
and bare shoulders, crepe streamers whirling me
under the lights. Chaperones beaming. I'd be a
nice boy again if I only had some Sen-Sen.

The Standing Broad Jump

Good at something, I practiced till I broke
the record by a foot. And then they said
forget it. "You think you're a grasshopper?
We haven't done that trick for twenty years."

Champion of the obsolete event,
I hook my toes on the board, spring forth,
and, just as I would fall, throw back my arms
and fly my whole ten feet to the measured sand.

The Annunciation

I.

Joe told Jane how the angel told
Mary not to be afraid
and then gave Jane another pull
on his bottle. Jane got laid

across the back seat of Joe's Ford
that Monday night above the town
when Joe informed her how the Lord
sent his favorite angel down

to Mary. "You're the Lord's handmaid,"
Joe told Jane the angel said:
"When Mary heard that, she obeyed
and followed where the angel led."

Joe gave Jane another gulp
of booze and, demonstrating how
the angel gave the Lord some help,
unbuttoned Jane and whispered, "Now

I'll tell you what I really think.
I think the whole thing was a fraud.
Pregnant, to avoid a stink,
she made it up, the clever broad.

But Jane said, "No," and took a drink,
and soon was saying, "God! Oh, God!"

II.

To the old park over San José,
Alum Rock, I come to find
the path where, as a college boy,
I took my sweethearts. In my mind

I ease my waxed and polished Ford.
Below, the yellow pins of light,
some still, some moving, mark the world,
and I and someone start the night.

When I switch the motor off,
first stillness, then the sough of trees,
then a million trills of life
in quiet level chorus rise.

Alone with someone with a name
to murmur, and to call my name,
I stir love up from its restless dream
and fashion it another time.

Is memory a fiction? Have
I made my life into a rhyme
of tricks and guilty luck, in love
with Joe and Jane in a drunken game?

Old give and take, old God, old slave,
old line that worked too well. Old shame.

III.

Joe tells Jane how the angel told
Mary not to be afraid.
Jane smiles and takes another pull
on their bottle. Joe has prayed

he'll work Jane to a helpless lather
this Monday night above the town
in his Ford when he tells her how the Father
sent the persuading angel down

to Mary. "You're the Lord's handmaid,"
Joe tells Jane the angel said.
"And now you'll tell me Mary made
the angel carry her to bed?"

Jane says and takes another gulp
of booze and, demonstrating how
Mary gave the Lord some help,
unzippers Joe and whispers, "Now,

I'll tell a tale we both can handle.
I know the whole affair was human.
Pregnant, to avoid a scandal,
she made it up, your clever woman.

But if I were told to wed the Lord,
I'd want my church to be your Ford."

IV.

It is a level patch of ground
between two trees. I'll call her Jane
again. A whisky flask, a moon,
a blanket, and no sign of rain—

Pacific spring—, and by the book
I woo and gain each inch of skin
beneath each buttonhole and hook
and eye and cup until I win,

or think I've won, what I am for.
Yet, having glided down the stair
of love, Jane cowers at the door,
giving up to a rush of tears

—or rash, or downpour. Is it fright
or whisky? Moral reprimand?
I heed the warning, end the night,
and lose her. Who could understand

love's throes on such an early date?
Many others, I supposed,
knew how to answer. I knew late
if at all, while I was raised

in the mysteries, from mate to mate,
by God's truth constantly amazed.

The Hawk

Driving to town this morning, I saw it
circling purposefully above a mown field.
I thought of its fine telescopic lenses
and the wee white-breasted mouse that would never look up.
The wings were a functional glory as they quivered
to fix the glide. I left it turning, turning.

You returned from work full of news
of arcs in late sunlight, the barred brown feathers
leaning in currents as it climbed and fell
and rose to the neighboring hill. Somewhere,
you knew, it settled to a limb to wait
the night out like a lonely, exiled king.

Could we, my love, have seen the same hawk?

... The Aepyornis egg compares to the hummingbird egg
as the largest whale compares to a medium-sized dog;
while the hummingbird egg, in turn, compares to the
human ovum as the largest whale compares to a large rat.

ISAAC ASIMOV

Compare

Aepyornis of Madagascar, elephant bird
with your foot-long, two-gallon egg
that would take two hours to hard boil
and could feed a congress of ornithologists,
look up to the hummingbird, who can fly
and, furthermore, still exists. Loaded,
you gave up your title to the ostrich.
Anyway, think of that puny half-inch egg.
Compared to yours, it is almost nothing,
not even a bite for my medium-sized dog
Barkus, supposing I did hard boil it in about ten seconds.
But if you ever start feeling classy, Aepyornis,
think of the largest whale, who could swallow whole
an Aepyornis about as easily as Barkus could swallow
a hummingbird egg if he ever got such fancy ideas.
And Barkus, you might get thinking yourself better
than an Aepyornis egg because you can run around.
You're not much, even compared to a hummingbird,
whose egg, compared to a human ovum, is like a whale
compared to a large rat, whom you couldn't catch.
Ovum, with no white and no yolk
to hard boil, and with only half a nucleus
at best, don't worry about anything.
The whale can't see you yet, and neither can my dog
or the hummingbird, and Aepyornis is all gone.
We know you are, really, beyond compare.
Be patient, an angel may visit you
with wonderful news: "You, from all the others. . . ."

Clay

When I began making clay figures,
my family ran from the house crying,
"He has the Gift! Look at his eyes!"
I looked at my eyes but saw nothing surprising.
I'd had the Gift all along, I decided, but no one
had really looked in my eyes until that moment,
and then partly to keep from looking at the clay people.

There were three: a young woman of ample but neat body
with a serious, practical face; and two children
with little pot bellies and skinny legs.
I kept smoothing their skin,
which got to look more and more real,
and I set them on the table together, with the woman
between the two children, all of them facing me.

I thought I noticed a faint reflex in the woman's right leg,
but I knew I was getting tired, so I just sat back
and looked at my work. Then I saw the big toe
on the same leg jerk, and the whole foot
spread and grab at the air,
after which things happened fast. All three
stood and shook themselves and got down off the table.

Then the woman knelt between the children,
gathered one in each arm, and spoke:
"Look closely at this man, especially at his eyes.
He is in reality a kind of monster.
He will look at you lovingly, his eyes cloudless pools,

and all the while he will be seeing you in your coffin,
and he will watch himself create you, minute by minute."

Then she took up the children, turned and went out.
On the front lawn, neighbors were gathering,
muttering with my family, pointing at the house.
The clay figures walked away, in their nakedness.

The Change

The wife has painted the bedroom floor, and tonight
they are downstairs in the study, in the pull-out bed
next to the sliding glass door. Beyond the deck
and back lawn their land climbs to a wood
and then a meadow. The world is awash in moonlight
so that from the clear dark cloud of the pear tree
plainly hangs the rope, still, where her boys
swung and laughed and landed, in those early days.
With her sleeping husband she lies in the bed and sees
the smoothed, long-shadowed moonlit land they own,
the room, too, full of a quiet glamour
that falls across the book shelves and the table,
out across the blankets and the floor
and deck and lawn and up into the trees
like a dream of gardens and assurances
well-painted and alive.
                         And then a cry
floats to her from out of the night somewhere,
rising cold in the glassed-out shining wind
a long moment, a thin bleating baby call
a rabbit makes when caught by a cat or a fox,
makes once, one time, only that once.

Thebes Revisited

"The question seems unfair," I said. "Could you
accept two out of three? Maybe, four legs
in the morning and two at noon, or two at noon
and three in the evening?" "Shut up," said the Sphinx.
"All or nothing." "Well," I said, "you don't
look unreasonable. You have a lovely, honest
face, and the way you keep lashing your tail—
all that power and determination. You're too strong
to be inflexible." The crescent needles
retracted a little into her great paws.
"A drunk might be on all fours in the morning
and up on two legs by noon," I said. "Wait,
I know that's wrong. I don't function well under pressure."
"You *are* warm," said the Sphinx. "Try to relax,
and think both literally and metaphorically.
You are sort of close when you say a drunk.
I don't want to give it away, but a drunk
is one category within the general classification
we're after. A drunk is a . . . what?" The terrible wings
unfurled, blocking the sun. "Cool down a minute,"
she said, "and just let your mind float.
A drunk is a . . ." "*Man,*" I said. "That's right,"
she said, "but you have to show how you got
the answer. You have to tie it to the question."
"Well, in the morning of his life, a man's a baby
and crawls on all fours," I said. "You're *good,*"
she said. "Now, part two." "He's up on his feet through life,"
I said, "but what about three legs? He's on
a football team, in a three-point stance, and they play
night football!" "You idiot," said the Sphinx,
gathering to spring. "It's an old guy with a cane.
I'm going to eat you." "Wait," I said. "A cane?
We don't use canes much now. An old man

might use a wheelchair. The question should read,
'What's on four legs in the morning, two at noon, and
on wheels at night?'" The noise within the walls
dwindled, and the city slept. The lone and level
sands stretched far away. "If that's how you see it,"
she said, head on her paws, "I'll have to let you pass."

NOTE

"Jazz for Kirby." Kirby Walker was a Harlem-born singer and piano man. In the 1930s he played with many fine jazz musicians, made a few records for Bluebird, and traveled in England and Europe as an entertainer and jazz pianist. During the 1940s he was back in New York, playing at The Famous Door and at other jazz spots on 52nd Street. In the early 1950s he appeared on the Arthur Godfrey Talent Scouts program on radio and won first prize, which was followed by a contract with Columbia Records and also a series on Keynote Records with Leonard Feather. Kirby moved upstate to Walton, New York, built a house there, and began appearing in nearby Oneonta at Jerry's Lounge. I met him there in 1959, and we worked together for six years. During his residence upstate he was visited by Louis Armstrong, J. C. Higgenbotham, Jimmy Rushing, Buster Bailey, Coleman Hawkins, Ben Webster, and other famous jazz artists. There were wonderful Sunday afternoon jam sessions. Kirby finally moved to New Jersey and opened a restaurant. I last saw him in 1968 when he returned to Oneonta for a two-week appearance with Slam Stewart. Kirby died a few years later.

The character developed in the poem is based mostly upon my experiences with Kirby, and partly upon Joe Lee Wilson, a black American singer I knew in Brighton, England. Some of Kirby's remarks in the poem were inspired by details and conversations recorded in Martin Williams' *Jazz Panorama* (Collier Books, 1964).

Richard Frost has published two books of poems *(The Circus Villains* and *Getting Drunk with the Birds)* with Ohio University Press. During the last forty years his poems have appeared in *TriQuarterly, Paris Review, Poetry, Harper's Magazine, Georgia Review,* and many other journals. He has won the Poetry Society of America's Gustav Davidson Memorial Award and has held a CAPS fellowship and an NEA creative writing fellowship. Frost is a working jazz drummer and is Professor of English at the State University College, Oneonta, New York.

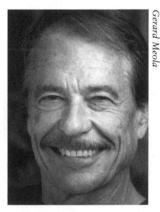

Gerard Meola